This book belong

Paperback ISBN: 978-1-63731-698-6
Hardcover ISBN: 978-1-63731-700-6
eBook ISBN: 978-1-63731-699-3

Printed and bound in the USA.
NinjaLifeHacks.tv

Ninja Life Hacks®
by Mary Nhin

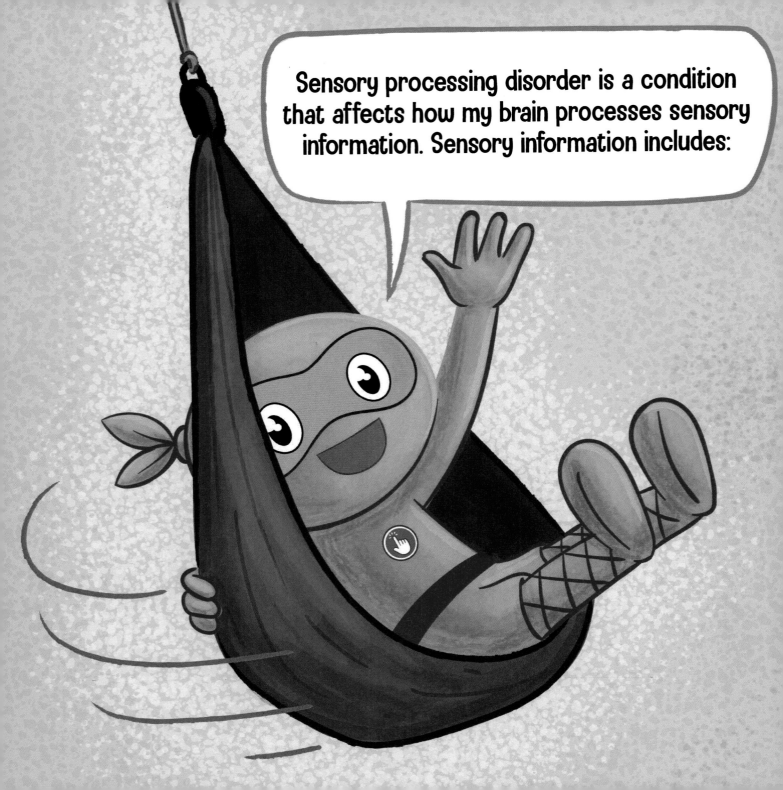

It's important for me to touch different textures like when I rub the silky part of my blanket at night. It helps to soothe me.

Other times, I am sensitive to touch. While I get goosebumps with an accidental bump or brush, I may not notice smaller things like hairs brushing the side of my face.

I also struggle with my balance so you may see me in constant motion and knock into things to feel more anchored.

Then one day, Calm Ninja introduced me to something called a Sensory Diet. It helps me meet my sensory needs, but it also helps me find my center when I'm triggered.

Continue the learning with our fun lesson plans which include superpower skills practice, STEM activity, craft, and more!

ninjalifehacks.tv

Ninja Life Hacks™

Sensory diets are a strategy to address sensory needs. In 1984, Patricia Wilbarger coined the term "sensory diet" to explain how certain sensory experiences can help a person's performance and help to remedy the disruption of their sensory processing systems. A sensory diet is a way to adjust sensory input relative to an individual's needs.

SENSORY DIET GRAPH

Practice yoga or exercise.

Eat foods with texture or crunchy.

Wrap myself in a blanket burrito/cuddle swing.

Listen to calming music.

Use a fidget toy while being read to or listening.

Go swimming or soak in a bath.

Jump on a trampoline.

Bounce on a yoga ball.

Sit in a wobble chair.

Wear a weighted vest.

Swing or play in the park.

Play with sensory bins.

Made in the USA
Middletown, DE
13 October 2023

40765985R00020